Fast Food & Franchising
A Beginner's Guide to Quick Service Restaurants

TJAART KRUGER

Copyright © 2018 Tjaart Kruger

All rights reserved.

ISBN: **1725669463**
ISBN-13: **978-1725669468**

DEDICATION

To the men and women of fast food. You truly are the hardest working and most underappreciated heroes of the food industry.

CONTENTS

1	Glossary	Pg 1
2	What is QSR?	Pg 3
3	To Franchise Or Not To Franchise	Pg 5
4	Do Your Homework	Pg 10
5	The 5 Key Points Of A Successful QSR Business	Pg 26
6	Basic Operations	Pg 40

FOREWORD

Are you ready to buy your first fast food franchise but you have no idea what to expect? Do you need some help understanding what is required and how to do certain things? This book will give you all the information you need to not only help you decide between franchising and not franchising, but also what key aspects to pay attention to so that you can do things the right way from the start. QSR is hard work, but with time can become very rewarding and profitable.

This book takes you step by step through the process of making your decision. Once you are the proud owner of the franchise or wholly-owned business that suits you, the book will continue to guide you through the maze of daily management, so that you can always be one step ahead of your target and your competition.

The author has made a few mistakes, learnt a lot, and guided numerous satisfied franchisees through the process. Follow this guide to the letter and you will enjoy your profits.

1 GLOSSARY

AOD – Admission of Debt: A contractually stipulated document signed by a cashier that allows you to legally hold them responsible for any cash shortages they may have incurred while performing their duties as a cashier..

BFF - Business Format Franchising: gives a franchisee the opportunity to make use of the franchisor's trademark and brand, as well as all the benefits that come with trading under its umbrella.

COS - Cost of Sales: What it cost to produce the turnover achieved.

CS - Closing Stock: The value of the stock at the end of the trading period.

FA - Franchise Agreement: A comprehensive contractual agreement that clearly stipulates the rights and privileges of both the franchisor and the franchisee in terms of the brand, registered trademarks and all other associated intellectual properties.

FSR - Full Service Restaurants: sit-down eateries where the food comes directly to the customer's table.

GP - Food Cost Gross Profit: Directly inverse to the cost of sales, this is the gross profit that was generated.

LSM - Living Standards Measurement: A uniquely South African way to determine and group the different market sector demographics.

OC - Operational Cost: Commonly referred to as overheads, this represents all costs to the business that do not form part of the Cost of Sales.

OS - Opening Stock: The value of the stock at time of commencement of the trading period.

POS - Point of Sale system: Commonly referred to as the till system.

PU – Purchases: Any raw materials purchased and used to produce a product for sale. Some exceptions may apply such as cleaning chemicals or any other purchases that do not directly form part of a recipe.

QSR - Quick Service Restaurants: Commonly referred to as Takeaway Restaurants.

RSP – Recommended Sales Price: As determined by the franchisor. Not so much a recommendation but rather the determined sales price to be implemented strictly and consistently.

SAARF – South African Audience Research Foundation: The source of the LSM framework included in this book.

SWOT - Strengths, Weaknesses, Opportunities, Threats: A method used to analyze a specific situation and use the different answers to the questions asked to determine an optimal course of action.

UC - Unit Cost: The cost of a stock item, as determined by the most basic UOM.

UOM - Basic Unit of Measure: The basic way to record stock onto a POS in its most basic measurement, i.e. Liter (L), Kilogram (KG) *(substitute for Imperial measurement system, i.e. (LBS) if needed)*, Per Unit (Each).

2 WHAT IS QSR

DEFINITION OF QSR VS. FSR

While there are many different types of franchising models, this book deals exclusively with the Business Format Franchising (BFF) model, and more specifically, the Quick Service Restaurant model. The BFF model gives a franchisee the opportunity to make use of the franchisor's trademark and brand, as well as all the benefits that come with trading under its umbrella such as:

- Lower supply costs
- Established supply chains
- Training
- Uniformity
- Operational planning and implementation
- Business know-how
- Marketing, etc.

This means that you, as the franchisee, are required to adopt and maintain the framework as provided by the franchisor to not only provide the product as prescribed, but to do so in the way and at the level of quality that is specified. Only the products provided by the franchisor in its business model may be provided to a customer. You, as the franchisee, must adhere to the strictly controlled environment which the franchisor supplies through regular training, as well as operational and health and safety audits (among many other potential checks).

Examples of Business Format Franchising:
- McDonalds
- KFC
- Chicken Licken
- Chicken

To put this in simple terms, you must do as the franchisor tells you, when they tell you and how they tell you. For example: If the franchisor tells you that you may only use stock branded and licensed by the franchisor in its supply chain, then that is the only stock that you may use and nothing else.

Quick service restaurants (QSR), or fast food restaurants as they are better known, is defined as a specific type of restaurant that serves fast food with little to no table service. They include fast casual restaurants and catering trucks.

Full service Restaurants (FSR), are defined as sit-down eateries where the food comes directly to the customer's table.

3 TO FRANCHISE OR NOT TO FRANCHISE

Often the biggest question anyone who considers entering the takeaway market needs to answer for themselves, is whether to join an existing brand of franchise, or to go it alone. To answer this question, you need to consider several factors and do a thorough analysis.

While much of the information captured in this book is wholly applicable to both routes, this book is aimed at:
- Allowing you the opportunity to make an informed choice, and
- Providing you with a basic understanding of the different aspects of QSR management.

THE PROS AND CONS OF FRANCHISING

What is franchising? At its most basic level, franchising is a mutually beneficial or symbiotic relationship between two parties: the franchisee and the franchisor.

For such a relationship to work both parties must be able to communicate freely and regularly, be it in the form of:
- Information such as a monthly income statement report from the franchisee to the franchisor, or
- A regular newsletter from the franchisor to the franchisee.

There is far more to this relationship than:
- Just a Franchise Agreement (or contract), or
- A financial and operational relationship such as a monthly franchise fee or
- Regular visits by a representative of the franchisor to deliver a service or

- Making use of the marketing and distribution resources a franchisor would possess.

It is important to understand that the franchisor grants the franchisee the ability to do business, using its branding or trademark by implementing the business model within the brand's operational framework and trading in an agreed upon manner.

Advantages of Franchising:

- Working with a tried and tested brand and business model allows the franchisee to begin operating a business in a very short time, based on a tried and tested concept.

- Setting up a business is easy because the franchisor will ensure that every new franchisee receives effective and detailed training, both theoretically as well as practically, to ensure that the franchisee has all the necessary tools to be successful. This can also include assistance when negotiating a lease, supplying contractors and designs for shop-fitting, recruitment of suitable staff and the initial stocking up of the business.

- Continuous support from the franchisor will assist the franchisee with all operational matters, ensuring both the protection of the brand as well as the business of the franchisee. This will include ensuring that the franchisee produces the franchisor's products according to its prescribed quality, as well as reporting based on regular evaluations such as operational, hygiene and health and safety audits.

- Distribution and marketing are supplied by the franchisor to all the franchisees in its group and for the benefit of all. Even local advertising is undertaken by the franchisee, with the assistance of the franchisor, to improve their effectiveness in their own territories.

- It is easier to procure financing from banking institutions for someone who is new to the business when joining a franchise.

Disadvantages of franchising:

- Setup costs are higher because a franchisor will impose a strict minimum standard on shop-fitting and stock as well as equipment.

- Operational procedures are strictly enforced by the franchisor and based on proven methods of doing business and are not negotiable.

- Ill-advised decisions taken by the franchisor could affect the business of the franchisee in a negative way.

THE PROS AND CONS OF GOING IT ALONE

Advantages of going it alone:
- As the ultimate decision maker, the buck stops with you. Every decision you make, and its consequences, are yours to own.

- Tasks and challenges can be prioritized quickly and efficiently, especially when using the SWOT analysis method which will be discussed later in the book.

- You can apply as much time and resources as you can manage, with direct results.

- You can choose your own team with required skill sets and experience, allowing you to apply your human resources based on your own requirements.

- Apply direct judgement to all decisions: sites and franchisee selection – you can choose who, where, why and how.

The disadvantages of going it alone:
- With limited financial resources you are very much restricted to how much you can do to set up your business in the way that you want, and you may need to take your time to build up capital so that you can add on or change aspects with time.

- Quite often you need to get a second opinion from a trusted mentor, advisor or significant other.

- You need to handle any successes and failures on your own.

- You must rely entirely on your own positive energy and motivation to get things done. No one else will do it.

- You must manage any setbacks that may occur, especially any beyond your control.

- Convincing stake holders - banks, landlords, investors, would-be franchisees and suppliers - that your start-up will deliver.

- You must manage the constant pressure of having to prioritize challenges, as QSR is a very tough environment.

It is important to understand that there is a natural cycle that every franchisee or independent store owner goes through. This is called the Happiness Bell-curve and it looks like this:

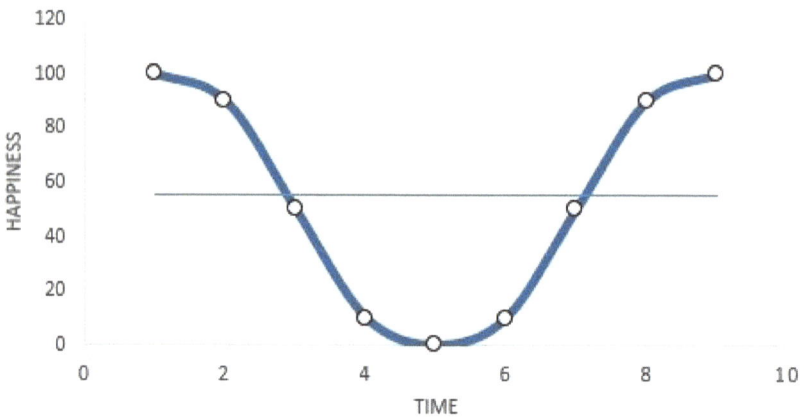

You will start off on top of the world at the time of the launch. As the business settles and the novelty wears off, business will show a slight downturn which will cause you concern. As you get to know your business you will undoubtedly begin to stress and worry and you will feel like you might have bitten off more than you can chew. At your lowest point you will want to kick yourself and ask "Why on earth did I ever decide to do this?".

But then you will pick yourself up and regain focus. You will learn to address each problem in an organized and structured manner and your confidence will return. As you solve each problem and things begin to smooth out, you will find yourself becoming more comfortable and ready for any challenges that come your way until, once again, you are on top of the world.

Remember that you are not omnipotent. Not everything is in your control. Sometimes things just happen and you will have to deal with it and this is where you will come to understand the kind of person you are and your own strengths.

The ability to confront a challenge, find a solution and to rise above it comes with time and experience. Later in the book we will discuss the SWOT analysis method of solving problems. This is by far the most effective way to deal with long-term challenges.

4 DO YOUR HOMEWORK

Do some leg work, whether you plan to join a franchise or go it alone. Always see what's out there, what's needed and how you can fill the gap effectively and make a difference. Most people considering entering the QSR environment always tend to look at the bigger, more well-known and established brands.

While these brands do have their advantages, going with a lesser-known brand comes with advantages of its own. Knowing which of these suits you better, or whether you would operate better on your own, is critical. You do not want to sign a contract that binds you for an extended period and be miserable because you made the wrong choice.

When you look at any brand, consider the following points:

- **Start-up costs:** The bigger, better-known brands tend to be more expensive because they bring more to the table but are also more rigid in their structure and level of control over their franchisees.

- **Profit margins:** You want to be able to make money.

- **Competition and market saturation:** Is there a gap you can fill with a product of your own, or that of an established franchise?

- **Location:** Location, Location, Location. Picking a profitable and strategically placed location cannot be stressed enough.

- **Level of support and reputation:** Research their online presence with tools such as Hello Peter or Trust Pilot and assess how the company manages complaints against them. Also find out as much as possible about the franchisors reputation amongst existing or ex-franchisees, as well as their reputation in the industry.

- **Training:** Do they provide an appropriate level of training based on your level of skill as a newcomer?

- **Unique selling point:** What makes them unique? What do they do better than anyone else?

- **LSM (Living Standards Measurement):** Are you catering to a market that can afford your product and make you profitable? (More on this will be discussed in the next chapter.)

- **Cultural requirements:** Will your product work on a cultural level within the catchment area you are looking at?

- **Age of franchise:** If the franchise you are considering is not a major brand, how long has the brand been around?

- **Sustainability:** Is this a fad franchise likely to disappear in a short period because it has run its course? Or does it have the potential to become a legitimate player in the industry?

LSM MARKET AND LOCATION

There are 10 different Living Standards Measurement (LSM) levels in South Africa. These are unique to the South African market, and are defined by the South African Audience Research Foundation (SAARF). The LSM index uses specific criteria to group people according to their standard of living, rather than using race, religion or other outmoded criteria. The most current version of the LSM standard in South Africa, at the time of publication, was last revised in 2012 and consisted of the following breakdown:

LSM 1 (2.1%)

DEMOGRAPHICS	MEDIA
Male and female 15 – 24 and 50+ Primary Completed Small urban/ Rural Traditional Hut R1 363 avg. household income per month GENERAL Minimal access to services Minimal ownership of durables, except radio sets Mzansi bank account Activities: minimal participation in activities, singing	Radio a major channel of media communication; mainly African Language Services (ALS)- Umhlobo **Wenene FM, Ukhozi FM and community**

LSM 2 (5.7%)

DEMOGRAPHICS	MEDIA
Female 15 – 24 and 50+ Some High School Small urban/ Rural Squatter Hut Shack, Matchbox and Traditional Hut R1 929 avg. household income per month GENERAL Communal access to water Minimal ownership of durables, except radio sets and stoves Mzansi bank account Activities: minimal participation in activities, singing	Radio: Commercial, mainly ALS- Ukhozi FM, Umhlobo Wenene FM

LSM 3 (6.5%)

DEMOGRAPHICS	MEDIA
Female 15 – 24 and 50+ Some High School Small Urban/ Rural Squatter Hut Shack, Matchbox and Traditional Hut R2 258 avg. household income per month **GENERAL** Electricity, water on plot or communal Minimal ownership of durables, except radio sets and stoves Mzansi bank account Activities – singing	Radio: Mainly ALS stations, Ukhozi FM, Umhlobo Wenene FM TV: SABC 1

LSM 4 (13.1%)

DEMOGRAPHICS	MEDIA
Male and female 15- 34 and 50+ Some High School Small Urban/ Rural Squatter Hut Shack, Matchbox and Traditional Hut R3 138 avg. household income per month **GENERAL** Electricity, water on plot or communal, non-flush toilet TV sets, electric hotplates Mzansi bank account Activities – attend gatherings, go to night clubs	Radio: Commercial mainly ALS, Gagasi, Motsweding, Ukhozi, Umhlobo Wenene FM, Community Radio TV: SABC 1

LSM 5 (16.9%)

DEMOGRAPHICS	MEDIA
Male 15-49 Some High School Small urban/ rural R4 165 avg. household income per month	Radio: Commercial mainly ALS stations, Lesedi FM, Motsweding FM, Ukhozi FM, community radio TV: SABC 1,2,3, e.tv, Daily Newspapers
GENERAL Electricity, water, flush toilet outside / communal TV sets, hi-fi/radio set, stove, fridge Mzansi accounts Activities: take away in past 4 weeks, bake for pleasure, go to night clubs, attend gatherings, buy lottery tickets	

LSM 6 (21%)

DEMOGRAPHICS	MEDIA
Male 25-49 Up to matric and higher Large Urban R6 322 avg. household income per month	Wide range of commercial and community radio TV: SABC 1,2,3, e.tv, Top TV, Community TV All print Outdoor
GENERAL Electricity, water in home, flush toilet in home Ownership of several durables plus cell phone Savings and Mzansi accounts Activities: hire DVDs, go to night clubs, take away in the past 4 weeks, attend gatherings, buy lottery tickets	

LSM 7 LOW (4.9%)

DEMOGRAPHICS	MEDIA
Female 25- 49 Matric and higher Urban R9 320 avg. household income per month	Wide range of commercial and community radio TV: SABC 1,2,3, e.tv, DStv, Top TV, Community TV All print Accessed internet past 7 days Cinema & Outdoor
GENERAL Full access to services Savings accounts Increased ownership of durables plus DVD and motor vehicle Participation in all activities	

LSM 8 LOW (4.3%)

DEMOGRAPHICS	MEDIA
Female 35+ Matric and higher Urban R13 210 avg. household income per month	Wide range of commercial and community radio TV: SABC 1,2,3, e.tv, M-Net, DStv, Top TV, Community TV All print Accessed internet past 7 days Cinema & Outdoor
GENERAL Full access to services and bank accounts Full ownership of durables, incl. PC Increased participation in activities	

LSM 8 HIGH (3.9%)

DEMOGRAPHICS	MEDIA
Male 35+ Matric and higher Urban R14 882 avg. household income per month	Wide range of commercial and community radio TV: SABC 2,3, e.tv, M-Net, DStv, Top TV, Community TV All print Accessed internet past 7 days Cinema & Outdoor
GENERAL Full access to services and bank accounts Full ownership of durables, incl. PC Increased participation in activities	

LSM 9 LOW (4.6%)

DEMOGRAPHICS	MEDIA
Female 35+ Matric and higher Urban R17 988 avg. household income per month	Wide range of commercial and community radio TV: SABC 2,3, e.tv, M-Net, DStv, Top TV, Community TV Accessed internet past 7 days All print Cinema & Outdoor
GENERAL Full access to services and bank accounts Full ownership of durables Increased participation in activities, excluding stokvel meetings	

LSM 9 HIGH (4.6%)

DEMOGRAPHICS	MEDIA
Male 35+ Matric and higher Urban R21 328 avg. household income per month	Wide range of commercial radio TV: SABC 2,3, e.tv, M-Net, DStv, Top TV, Community TV Accessed internet past 7 days All print Cinema & Outdoor
GENERAL Full access to services and bank accounts Full ownership of durables Increased participation in activities, excluding stokvel meetings	

LSM 10 LOW (3.3%)

DEMOGRAPHICS	MEDIA
Male 35+ Matric and higher Urban R26 706 avg. household income per month	Wide range of commercial radio TV: SABC 3, M-Net, DStv, Top TV, Community TV All print Accessed internet past 7 days Cinema & Outdoor
GENERAL Full access to services and bank accounts Full ownership of durables Increased participation in activities, excluding stokvel meetings	

LSM 10 HIGH (3.1%)

DEMOGRAPHICS	MEDIA
Male 35+ Matric and higher Urban R32 521 avg. household income per month	Wide range of commercial radio TV: M-Net, DStv, Community TV All print Accessed internet past 7 days Cinema & Outdoor
GENERAL Full access to services and bank accounts Full ownership of durables Increased participation in activities, excluding stokvel meetings	

While it may be somewhat out of date, especially in South Africa's rapidly changing demographic make-up, it is still a useful tool to determine if a specific area has the potential to be profitable, should you decide to open a store there. Below is a link to an automatic function that can help you make an informed decision for the South African market:

http://www.eighty20.co.za/lsm-calculator/

SWOT ANALYSIS

A SWOT analysis or SWOT matrix is a study undertaken by an organization to identify its internal strengths and weaknesses, as well as its external opportunities and threats.

This technique can be used in almost any decision-making situation to help identify the Strengths, Weaknesses, Opportunities, and Threats related to that situation. It helps to identify any positive or negative elements that could influence the decision's outcome, and indicates what the decision maker can improve on, or which facts or actions can be used to strengthen the situation.

A **SWOT** analysis shows exactly what its acronym stands for:
S - Strengths
W - Weaknesses
O - Opportunities
T – Threats

It is a set of questions one asks with a specific situation in mind, to determine the best possible way to come up with a solution. To begin with, the first two letters (Strengths and Weaknesses) work to cancel each other out, while the last two (Opportunities and Threats) do the same. There is almost no Weakness that does not have a corresponding and opposing Strength. Similarly, there is no Threat that cannot become an Opportunity. You just need to ask the right questions.

In this instance we will consider the question with two very simple examples:

SCENARIO 1: You have been offered a rental space at a fuel station in a rural location some 50km from the nearest town. The rental is extremely cheap and there is no other fast food business with which to compete. The average LSM ranges between 1 and 2 (See the LSM breakdowns in the previous chapter).

STRENGTHS	WEAKNESSES
• Cheap Rental • No competition within 50Km radius	• Very limited market • No prospects for high volume trade • Very low to no profitability
OPPORTUNITIES	THREATS
• Establish the brand	• Loss of investment • Real threat of incurring unpayable debts

CONCLUSION: This store should not be authorized for construction due to its very short predicted lifespan and lack of profitability due to its location and lack of a suitable market.

SCENARIO 2: You have been offered a rental space in a busy strip mall with a vibrant and growing LSM market that ranges between 4 and 8 (See the LSM breakdowns in the previous chapter). There is a high cultural demand for your product and general unhappiness with the existing options due to inconsistent quality and high prices.

STRENGTHS	WEAKNESSES
• Perfect location due to growing LSM market • Relatively low rental based on store size • Growing local demand for quality product at affordable prices • High levels of investment in local infrastructure • Store space meets all requirements in terms of power, drainage and water supply	• High crime area
OPPORTUNITIES	THREATS
• Extend brand image • Growing market • High cultural demand for product saturation	• Other competing brands

CONCLUSION: This store is perfectly placed in a growing market, is the right size with an affordable rental price and meets all infrastructure requirements. The area has a clear need of a quality product at affordable prices.

So, as you can see, it is all about asking the right questions and drawing a conclusion based on their answers. Now, as an exercise when asking the question – Is this the right location? - what would be your analysis and your conclusion?

POS OPTIONS

While most established franchises will have a preferred and prescribed Point of Sale system available with an accompanying database of recipes already set up, going it alone can be very challenging. Selecting the right Point of Sale system, and using it correctly, can be a real benefit for you. If you do decide to go it alone, take the lessons captured in this book to heart, as they will save you no end of pain if you approach matters in a structured and organized manner.

While most POS systems operate in a similar manner at their most basic level, each system will have advantages and disadvantages that will make them more or less attractive.

Advantages to look for:
- **Cost:** Can you afford the system? Consider the purchasing price, installation costs, monthly royalties, and the potential for upscaling when your business grows.
- **Relevance to your business:** You want a system that can cope with many transactions for different products every day, and a system designed for a retail environment will not do it for you.
- **Ease of use:** How easy is it to adapt the system to your specific needs?
- **Robust reporting:** Can you quickly extract useful reports?
- **Level of service supplied:** Can you get consistent, quick and affordable after-sales service?
- **Warranties and maintenance agreements:** How often are upgrades done? How long do you need to be off-line for upgrades? What do you do when there is unexpected downtime?

The list below shows some of the many options available in South Africa. Should you not be from South Africa, a simple search on the internet for your specific country should yield a multitude of systems available:
- Aloha POS - http://www.alohapos.co.za/
- GAAP - http://www.gaap.co.za/
- Galaxy POS - http://www.galaxypos.co.za/
- InTouch POS - https://intouchpos.co.za/
- Micros - http://www.micros.co.za/
- Postechdirect - http://www.postechdirect.co.za/
- PowerPos - http://www.powerpos.co.za/Home.aspx

EQUIPMENT

When considering equipment, it is always good to really do your homework. There are several factors that need to be considered when choosing an equipment supplier, the kind of equipment needed and what the supporting requirements are to make use of the equipment.

As is always the case, budget is important, but so is quality. Quite often, a franchisor (particularly the more established brands) will manage the entire process of procuring equipment and will include it as part of the turnkey investment, but this may not always be the case, especially if you decide not to join a franchise. It becomes a matter of quality versus affordability.

Here, again, is a good example of a question that can be evaluated using a SWOT analysis. Apply the analysis to each vendor you investigate. What are their strengths and weaknesses? What opportunities do they offer and what threat, if any, could manifest out of buying from them?

Remember, QSR is an electricity-hungry environment. Always consider the site's level of available infrastructure. Is enough electricity supplied to the main distribution board? Is 3-phase power required? Is the landlord willing to upgrade or allow you to hire an outside contractor to do so? Are there any specific turnkey requirements that need to be considered such as specialized adaptor fittings? There are many questions that can and need to be asked, so ask them.

In South Africa there are a few big players in catering equipment provision, servicing and manufacture. The best known of these are both manufacturers and importers:

- Foodserv - https://www.foodserv.co.za/
- Vulcan - https://vulcan.co.za/
- Omni Catering Manufacturers - http://www.omnicatering.co.za/
- MacBrothers - http://www.macbrothers.co.za/home.php

Again, find your own suppliers in your country and research their on-line reputation.

SHOPFITTING

Shopfitting can be a contentious and hazardous process. Finding the right contractor to fulfil your needs depends on several factors.

Firstly, the more expensive the contractor, the more likely they are to provide all aspects of shopfitting in-house. From plumbing to electrical to carpentry and construction, they will do it all, but you will pay for it.

Smaller outfits tend to subcontract to independent specialists, which can often lead to them losing control, which in turn may lead to the timeline falling by the wayside and costs ballooning. Without an ironclad agreement to ensure that the contractor takes full overall responsibility for the entire project, this can be a trying business.

It would also do well to find out who the contractor's big clients are. This will tell you if they understand aspects such as the installation of extraction systems, drainage and electricity, and if they have the requisite experience doing this kind of work. Remember, not all shopfitters do the same work. For example, some specialize in retail, while others specialize in hospitality installations. Always make sure to ask for references and follow up on them.

Make sure that you are fully aware of the terms they offer and what the payment percentages are. The norm tends to be 60 percent payment up front, 30 percent on completion and 10 percent to be paid once all snags are corrected.

A danger to be aware of is that the smaller guys often tend to drop the ball on the unprofitable aspects of the work, and sometimes will try to get more money from you to correct their mistakes. Again, make sure that you understand the terms of the installation agreement and ask questions until you are satisfied.

SUPPLIERS AND ACCOUNTS

Choosing the right suppliers can be a daunting task if you are not a part of a franchising group. The internet is a very good place to start looking, with many wholesalers maintaining an online presence. Take the time to do price comparisons. Study the terms and conditions, delivery schedules and payment options. It is always good to research a supplier.

Whether you are looking at a franchise or wholly owned business, make sure that you have enough capital available to cover not only the first opening order, but the next one as well. There's no telling how the launch will go, so it may take a bit of time to recoup the costs through sales. You will need to ensure that you can abide by the payment terms offered by your suppliers. In the QSR industry, this tends to range from Cash on Delivery (C.O.D) to 30-day payment plans, depending on the supplier and the product range. It is never a good idea to default or be late on payment, since a good working relationship with a supplier is essential to a healthy business.

STAFF RECRUITMENT AND TRAINING

Recruitment is a key factor to a healthy and well-functioning business. In the QSR industry appearance and communication are extremely important. Any employee, whether on the frontline of the business or otherwise, needs to be able to communicate well in both English and any other relevant native or regional language. They must be neatly groomed and always presentable, with vibrant personalities. Having experience in the relevant positions you hire them for is a bonus, but quite often not having experience can be even better, since you will have the opportunity to train them correctly without inheriting any bad habits.

Training should also be an ongoing process. Every shift should start with a briefing that not only entails the day's goals and specific work instructions, but some sort of training as well. This can take the form of roleplay, or just questions and answers. Every opportunity should be taken to ensure that your team is cross-trained as much as possible in the different areas of the store, to ensure that they are interchangeable should the need arise.

Always document any training done, and make sure that your team signs the document for future reference.

5 THE 5 KEY POINTS OF A SUCCESSFUL QSR BUSINESS

There are 5 key elements that together will give you the best chance at a successful QSR business:
- Quality Product
- Location
- Customer Service
- Marketing
- Stock Management

QUALITY PRODUCT

You will need to have a quality product to make an impression in the QSR market. It needs to fill a niche in the market that is either not being met but in demand, or not being met sufficiently according to demand. You can use a SWOT analysis to determine if joining a franchise with a specific product offering fills that gap or over-saturates it.

Do not be afraid of competition but be wary of over-saturation. Too much competition can also be detrimental. When you deliver a superior product with superior service at a reasonable price, you can overcome your competition. It is all about building your reputation.

LOCATION

Research your intended location. Does it comply with your requirements and also demand for the product you intend to deliver? What are the local cultural demands, if any, and who would be your competitors? Will the business be able to do decent trade 7 days a week or is it limited to a work week, i.e. Mondays to Fridays?

What is the income range of your intended market? Using the LSM calculator for this can be a good indicator but doing one-on-one surveys with people in the area will also help you gauge their need as well as their feelings towards your competitors and their short-comings.

CUSTOMER SERVICE

Cashiers are the faces of the QSR business and they need to be a cut above the rest. Good mathematical skills, fluency in both English and any other relevant local dialects, well-groomed appearances and outgoing, sparkling personalities are a must. Remember, they are the people who will represent your business on the frontline.

As management, you and your assistant manager or shift supervisor must tick all these boxes and more. You must have a flair for social interaction and be able to resolve conflict, both in-house and on the frontline. You also need to have a head for business.

Customer service is one of the most important factors in keeping a business healthy. How you treat your employees in front of customers, how you treat customers in front of your employees, and how you and your assistant or supervisor behave yourselves, will all reflect on the business and how customers perceive the value of the business.

MARKETING

As part of a franchise, you will have the benefit of making use of the franchisor's wide-spread reach. Younger brands tend to take longer to expand that reach, but it is essential that you as franchisee always give feedback on the effectiveness of the marketing campaigns that are put in place.

You should also do your best to focus on the needs of your own territory through rigorous and constant local marketing campaigns. These are usually the financial responsibility of the franchisee but done with the consent of the franchisor and implemented with the franchisor's help.

If you are an independent operator, rigorous and constant local marketing should be a given. Never give up on it. If a formula works, use it. If it doesn't, ask why it didn't, and what can you do differently to have a bigger impact?

Always make sure that you implement a marketing strategy that is measurable. Without a way to measure its effectiveness, how will you know if you're not just throwing good money after bad?

Use your recipe matrix (discussed later) to determine the products that are most in demand. Produce special offers that are based on these numbers so that you can give your customers more of what they want.

STOCK MANAGEMENT

Stock management is often the forgotten or misunderstood part of ensuring a successful business. In fact, as with each of the other points mentioned above, it can make or break you if not dealt with in an effective, well-managed and consistent manner.

One of the biggest mistakes franchisees almost always make is not to notice lack of uniformity when dealing with stock. It is essential that when dealing directly with stock, whether it is receiving, recipes or stock counting, it must be done in a consistent manner throughout.

- Stock management is divided into a few key but distinct elements:
- Receiving of stock and invoices
- Recipe Structuring
- Wastage
- Stock counts

Receiving of Stock and Invoices

Receiving stock into the store is a very important event. There are several factors that need to be accounted for:
- Always confirm that the correct delivery vehicle is used. Stock that needs to be frozen must be delivered with a refrigerated truck applying the correct temperature range. The stock must also not exhibit any signs of having defrosted previously, as this can be a potential health hazard.
- Always verify that what you ordered is what you receive. If the stock needs to be of a specific brand, quality or quantity and it is not the case, return it and demand correction. Make sure to note the issue on the delivery note copy retained by the delivery personnel as well as your own, to ensure that it cannot be disputed later. Remember to follow up on any previous returns or corrections, to ensure you get value for the service you pay for.
- Ensure all stock is secured in the correct holding environment as soon as it is delivered. Frozen stock must go into a freezer or freezer room, refrigerated products into a refrigerator, and dry stock into a dry store.
- Ensure that any packaging delivered to you is dry and in perfect

condition. If you are a franchisee, ensure that the packaging is correctly branded.
- When receiving stock onto the Point of Sale, make sure that you enter the stock correctly. As a franchisee you will receive instruction on the standards accepted by the franchisor. As an independent operator, keep things as simple as possible. Reduce your stock from pack sizes down to the most basic Unit of Measure (UOM) such as Kilogram (KG), Litre (L) or Each.
- Make sure you focus on line item by line item on the delivery note. Once an item has been received, tick it off and move on to the next line item.
- Double check the stock quantities received and values of the line items on the delivery note.
- Ensure that you pay attention to tax values. If the item is a non-taxable item, ensure that it is captured as such.
- Double check the total value of the delivery note, including the total tax value. Your bookkeeper will thank you for it.
- Always file your delivery note and write on them the date they were received onto the system. That way you can refer back if something has gone wrong.
- Ensure you receive the ENTIRE delivery note, and separately note on the delivery note any stock sent back due to incorrect deliveries. Once you fully received the items on the delivery note, issue a credit note through the POS's credit note function to correct any short-delivered stock. That way you have a digital record of what occurred, and you will always know what the circumstances were when the invoiced items were delivered.

Uniformity is extremely important. There must be a consistent and uniform manner in which the stock is handled from beginning to end. How stock is received is determined by the recipe, and this also determines how your stock must be counted.

Let's look at the example below to demonstrate uniformity and conversion:

Fresh 'n Fun Bakery

Street Address	P: 011-123-4567	freshnfunbakery@gmail.com
City, State ZIP Code	F: 011-890-1234	www.FreshnFunBakery.com

Bill To: Funky Chicken Roodepoort
Address: Shop 3, Sellyousoulforashop Mall, Roodepoort, 1790
Phone: 011-111-2222
Fax: 011-111-3333
Email: funkychickenrdpt@gmail.com
Invoice #: 0001239858
Invoice Date: 15-06-2018

Invoice For:

Item #	Description	Qty	Unit Price	Discount	Price
1	Burger Buns (6pck)	12	R 1,50	R -	R 18,00
2	Hotdog Rolls (6pck)	10	R 1,25		R 12,50
3	Cocktail Rolls (36pck)	5	R 0,25		R 1,25
4	Loaf White	3	R 12,00		R 36,00
5	Loaf Brown	5	R 10,00		R 50,00
6	Loaf Whole Wheat	3	R 15,00		R 45,00
					R -
					R -
					R -
					R -
					R -
				Invoice Subtotal	R 162,75
				Tax Rate	15,00%
				Sales Tax	R 24,41
				Other	
				Deposit Received	
				TOTAL	R 187,16

Make all checks payable to Fresh 'n Fun Bakery.
Total due in 7 days. Overdue accounts subject to a service charge of <#>% per month.

- The Burger Buns are received in packs of 6 and you have received 12 packs. Reducing this to the most basic UOM, you will be receiving 72 Burger Buns at a total value of R18.00 excluding tax.
- The Hotdog Rolls are received in packs of 6 and you have received 10 packs. Reducing this to the most basic UOM, you will be receiving 60 Hotdog Rolls at a total value of R12.50 excluding tax.
- The Cocktail Rolls are received in packs of 36 and you have

received 5 packs. Reducing this to the most basic UOM, you will receive 180 Cocktail Rolls at a total value of R1.25 excluding tax.

The loaves can be entered in one of two ways, depending on how the recipe is set up.
- If we accept that a single loaf gives 18 slices and the recipe deducts 2 slices per sale:
- The Loaf White is received as 18 slices and you have received 3 loaves. Reducing this to the most basic UOM, you will receive 54 slices at a total value of R36.00 excluding tax.
- The Loaf Brown is received as 18 slices and you have received 5 loaves. Reducing this to the most basic UOM, you will receive 90 slices at a total value of R50.00 excluding tax.
- The Loaf Whole Wheat is received as 18 slices and you have received 3 loaves. Reducing this to the most basic UOM, you will receive 54 slices at a total value of R45.00 excluding tax.
- If we accept that a loaf gives 18 slices and the recipe deducts 0.0555 per sale:
- The Loaf White is received as 1 loaf and you have received 3 loaves. Reducing this to the most basic UOM, you will receive 3 loaves at a total value of R36.00 excluding tax.
- The Loaf Brown is received as 1 loaf and you have received 5 loaves. Reducing this to the most basic UOM, you will receive 5 loaves at a total value of R50 excluding tax.
- The Loaf Whole Wheat is received as 1 loaf and you have received 3 loaves. Reducing this to the most basic UOM, you will receive 3 loaves at a total value of R45.00 excluding tax.

As you can see, it is important to take the way the recipe works into account.

- Double check each line item on the delivery note for quantity and value and compare to quantity and value received onto the POS.
- Double check the Invoice Subtotal on the invoice against the subtotal on the POS.
- Double check the total Sales Tax on the Invoice against the total on the POS.
- Double check the inclusive total against the total on the POS. There may be some slight difference due to the tax rounding function of the system, but this should not exceed more than 3

or 4 cents.
- Only once you are completely satisfied that the invoice is correct, finalize it.

RECIPES AND THE RECIPE MATRIX

If you are a franchisee, the franchisor will oversee the recipe matrix. From updating the recipe breakdown to the Recommended Sales Price (RSP), to the expected GP and the maintenance of all of this on the Point of Sale system, the franchisor should be in control.

If you are an independent operator though, this will be your job. Use a spreadsheet to keep an independent record of your recipes, the cost of each ingredient, the overall cost of the recipe, the sales price and consequent GP of the produced product.

The recipe matrix is a very intricate and complex tool, encompassing all the information that helps you determine the theoretical GP, analyze sales trends and build a menu that is both in demand and properly structured.

The first step to building a matrix is to list each recipe, the recipe's ingredients and their costings. You can list the ingredients on a separate tab where you can keep record of the negotiated prices and have that information pull through to the recipe tab. In this way you only ever need to update the price of any ingredient once to update the costings of every recipe.

You can then create a menu tab where you can have a summary of the menu items based on the recipe tab, along with the cost of sales for each menu item, the theoretical GP, and of course the sales price – part of the calculation to determine the GP.

Try not to increase sales prices more than once every six months at the most. Changing prices too often can confuse customers and often scare them off.

You can also use each menu item's GP to determine your overall theoretical GP by determining the average.

WASTE AND WASTE MANAGEMENTAND

There are two types of wastage: raw and recipe-based. Every fit for purpose POS system can deal with both types, but a lot depends on how the recipes are loaded onto the system. All QSR-based POS systems can call on a recipe within a recipe. This is called nesting.

I would also suggest using an easily recognizable naming convention when creating a nested recipe. As an example, see below:

Fast Food & Franchising
A Beginner's Guide to Quick Service Restaurants

Nested Recipe — NR - CHICKEN BURGER SPICY

Item	Unit	Qty	Cost	Total
Chicken Breast Fillet 5kg	KG	0,12	R42,29	R5,07
Oil Palmolein	L	0,0204	R17,93	R0,37
Spicy Breading (5Kg)	KG	0,0233	R43,54	R1,01
CHEESE EASY SLICE 16.7G EACH	EACH	1	R1,21	R1,21
Lettuce	KG	0,02	R14,95	R0,30
Tomato	KG	0,025	R12,95	R0,32
CX Creamy Mayo	KG	0,021	R35,40	R0,74
Sesame Seed Burger Bun	EACH	1	R2,75	R2,75
			Total	R11,79

Container Recipe — CHICKEN BURGER SPICY

Item	Unit	Qty	Cost	Total
NR - CHICKEN BURGER SPICY	Each	1	R11,79	R11,79
Branded Wax Wrapper 30x33cm	EACH	1	0,168	0,168
1 Ply 300x300 Serviette	EACH	2	0,123	0,246
S08 Brown Bag 500	EACH	0,5	0,52648	0,26324
			Total	R12,46

As you can see, there are two recipes. One is the container recipe (or raw stock) as it will appear on the POS screen and printed receipts – **CHICKEN BURGER SPICY**, and the second is the nested recipe – **NR – CHICKEN BURGER SPICY**, separating the product from the accompanying condiments e.g. a serviette and wax wrapper.

The reason for doing it this way is simple. Raw stock is exactly that. It is stock that is used to produce the product, but if for some reason the raw stock can no longer be used, it needs to be discarded. This can simply be captured as wastage.

Recipe-based wastage is more complex, because you are now dealing with a finished product that encompasses several individual stock items with specific quantities. Using the POS system's recipe-based wastage function, you will record the wastage by logging the nested recipe, not the container recipe. That way you only write off the actual waste, and not the accompanying packaging and other non-edible items that can still be used.

Failing to properly implement this from the start can cause real headaches later when you are trying to balance your stock.

Your POS system will also supply you with reporting that can be used to manage your waste, so that you limit your losses by implementing better production planning.

A great example of a POS system that has all these features is the GAAP Point of Sale.

STOCK COUNTS

Stock counting is one of the most misunderstood and most important aspects of running a QSR business. It is often neglected or ignored, when it should be rigidly enforced and thoroughly analyzed on a regular and consistent basis.

Best practice suggests doing regularly scheduled stock counts at three intervals: Daily, Weekly and Monthly. Often the weekly and monthly stock count is one and the same. It should be noted that the monthly stock count is quite possibly the most important one as it sets the tone for the next month, although this should not subtract in any way from the other two types.

A daily stock count should reconcile your core stock items and include all perishables. A weekly and monthly stock count should be a comprehensive stock count, considering every stock item in the store.

Please do not include cleaning chemicals, as these are considered operational costs - they are not directly related to the production or sale of a product.

Also, remember that a monthly stock count is completed on the last trading day of the month after the close of business. The closing stock determined by this stock count – once you have thoroughly investigated any irregularities before finalizing the stock count – becomes the opening stock for the next month and cannot be changed or influenced for the whole of the next trading month. Getting it wrong means, you will have 30 days to cry before you can even begin to fix it, and then only by doing another month end stock count.

The following is a basic formula for doing a weekly / monthly stock count. The principles are as applicable to daily stock counts as weekly/monthly stock counts:

PREPARATION

1. Schedule the weekly stock count to occur on the quietest weekly day of trade.
2. Ensure all invoices have been captured and verified as correct.
3. Ensure that the stock sheet contains all stock items required by editing it if possible and confirming that all relevant stock items have been selected.
4. Ensure that you have a kitchen scale in a fully working condition available.
5. Ensure that the staff on the closing shift are aware that they will take part in the stock count and will be held accountable for any stock in their sections.
6. **Store Room** (to be done well before actual stock count occurs)
    a. Where possible, try to ensure that:
        i. Any packaging bales or bulk stock of a similar nature that have been opened have been moved to

the relevant kitchen area, leaving only sealed bales in the store

OR

  ii. Any packaging bales or bulk stock of a similar nature that have been opened have been counted and portioned, i.e.:
    1. Burger Boxes in multiples of 50 and secured together by an elastic band
    2. Medium and Large Paper bags in multiples of 50 and secured together by an elastic band
  iii. All identical stock items are stored together and not spread all over the store room

7. **Freezer Room** (to be done well before actual stock count occurs)
    a. Ensure the Freezer Room is packed neatly and in a logical fashion that will make counting easy.
    b. Any opened product (cardboard packaging) such as frozen chips should have the top lids removed to allow for quick identification and easy counting.
8. **Cold Room** (to be done well before actual stock count occurs)
    a. Ensure the Cold Room is packed neatly and in a logical fashion that will make counting easy and that all containers are labelled and dated.

PROCESS
1. Roughly one hour before the store closes – and only if trading allows – the manager can begin to count and record the store room contents.
2. The freezer room contents may be counted, weighed and recorded next, and must include any product removed for defrosting.
3. The Cold Room contents may be counted, weighed and recorded next.
4. Once completed, no further stock may be issued unless recorded and deducted from the completed count,
5. At the point in the evening when the kitchen has been cleaned and no longer produces, the cookers and any burger section employees need to start counting, weighing and recording,

6. Once the store has closed and the last of the customers have been assisted and have left the premises, frontline staff need to follow through with their cleaning duties and only then begin to count any stock that may be in their section and under their control.
7. During this time all remaining cashiers must be cashed up and all necessary processes followed, but the End of Day procedure **MAY NOT BE COMPLETED ON THE POINT OF SALE UNTIL AFTER THE STOCK COUNT HAS BEEN FINALISED.**
8. Once all sections have been counted, the figures must be tallied and entered into the point of sale system as required.

ANALYSIS

1. All unexplained variances must be investigated and, if necessary, the stock in question must be recounted and verified by the relevant staff as well as the manager on duty.
2. Once this is done, and only if the manager on duty is satisfied that all the information captured is 100% correct, may the stock count be finalised.
3. The stock count record as well as the physical counts recorded must be filed for future reference in a stock file and must be kept on record for at least 2 months.

INCOME STATEMENT

The Income Statement or Profit and Loss Statement is an invaluable tool to help you determine the health and financial state of your business. Completing the income statement at the end of every month and analyzing it thoroughly should be a habit.

Below are two examples of income statements or Profit and Loss statements. First, let's look at an example of a bad income statement.

In the example below we can see that the turnover (A) amounted to R310 678. While this may look fantastic, we are not done yet. Looking at the Opening Stock (B) we can see that it is excessively high and may indicate that when the previous month ended that there was not sufficient care taken to limit and reduce purchases. It could also be an indicator that the final stock count for the previous month was not quite accurate and there may be stock inflation involved. Remember, this value is determined by the final stock count's Closing Stock value.

FUNKY CHICKEN
LOCATION: Roodepoort

STATEMENT OF PROFIT AND LOSS FOR THE PERIOD : June 2018

Revenue	310 678,00	A	
- Cost of Sales	264 679,00		
Opening Stock	101 653,00	B	
+ Purchases	84 567,00		
- Closing Stock	78 459,00		
Gross Profit	45 999,00	C	14,81%
Operating Expenses	79 622,18		
	-		0,00%
Accounting fee	1 980,00		0,64%
Bank charges	4 224,20		1,36%
Cleaning	1 549,40		0,50%
Consulting & Legal	5 263,16		1,69%
Electricity and water	11 339,91		3,65%
Franchise Fees	10 809,83		3,48%
Franchise Advertising	3 242,95		1,04%
General	-		0,00%
Insurance	709,95		0,23%
Local Advertising & Promotion	1 232,11		0,40%
POS	4 057,79		1,31%
Print/Stationary/Post	84,43		0,03%
Rent	11 675,44		3,76%
Repairs & Maintenance	460,53		0,15%
Salaries & Wages	19 323,43		6,22%
Security	271,93		0,09%
Staff training	-		0,00%
Telephone & Fax	1 840,17		0,59%
Transport & Vehicle expenses	1 556,95		0,50%
Uniforms	-		0,00%
Operating Profit/(Loss)	-33 623,18	D	
Estimated Income tax	-	E	
Net Profit/(Loss) After Tax	R -33 623,18		

We can also see that the Gross Profit (C) for the food cost only is already very low when we take into account all of the Operating Expenses. To be profitable, you need to understand what your operating expenses are, and which of them are stable values that do not change from one month to the next, or rarely do so.

In this case the Operating Expenses are far more than the Gross Profit, leaving the statement short on profit by almost R34 000. Based on this Income Statement, I would explore the following:

- Was the previous month's stock count correct?
- Were all the purchasing invoices correctly captured?
- Was the latest stock count done correctly since the GP% is extremely low?
- Based on the stock reports, are there any serious issues that need to be addressed to prevent any further losses?

There are numerous reasons why an income statement can look like this. The key is to continuously analyze the information, find solutions, and implement them consistently and effectively with the help of the daily stock counts as well as the stock report for the month to date.

Now let's look at an example of a good income statement. Here we can see that the turnover is very good. The opening stock and closing stock are nice and low and the Gross Profit is more than sufficient to cover the Operating Expenses.

Always try to ensure that your rental does not exceed 10% of your turnover. Salaries and wages should also not exceed 10% of the turnover. These two should be the highest individual expenses for the store, with water and electricity in third place.

Also, the reason why there is no tax indicated on this statement is because we are working in its entirety with values after tax.

Fast Food & Franchising
A Beginner's Guide to Quick Service Restaurants

FUNKY CHICKEN
LOCATION: Roodepoort

STATEMENT OF PROFIT AND LOSS FOR THE PERIOD : June 2018

Revenue	394 678,00	A	
- Cost of Sales	208 679,00		
Opening Stock	69 653,00	B	
+ Purchases	84 567,00		
- Closing Stock	54 459,00	C	
Gross Profit	185 999,00	D	47,13%
Operating Expenses	88 546,25		
	-		0,00%
Accounting fee	1 980,00		0,50%
Bank charges	4 224,20		1,07%
Cleaning	1 549,40		0,39%
Consulting & Legal	5 263,16		1,33%
Electricity and water	11 339,91		2,87%
Franchise Fees	19 733,90	E	5,00%
Franchise Advertising	3 242,95		0,82%
General	-		0,00%
Insurance	709,95		0,18%
Local Advertising & Promotion	1 232,11		0,31%
POS	4 057,79		1,03%
Print/Stationary/Post	84,43		0,02%
Rent	11 675,44		2,96%
Repairs & Maintenance	460,53		0,12%
Salaries & Wages	19 323,43	F	4,90%
Security	271,93		0,07%
Staff training	-		0,00%
Telephone & Fax	1 840,17		0,47%
Transport & Vehicle expenses	1 556,95		0,39%
Uniforms	-		0,00%
Operating Profit/(Loss)	97 452,75	G	
Estimated Income tax	-		
Net Profit/(Loss) After Tax	R 97 452,75		

6 BASIC OPERATIONS

OPENING CHECKLIST

- On arrival at the store, first confirm that none of the entrances have been compromised during your absence. Should you observe anything suspicious, immediately contact your designated security company or the authorities.
- Enter the store, confirming that you close and lock the door behind you until the first staff member on duty arrives.
- Test any defrosting stock using your probe thermometer to ensure that the full defrosting cycle has completed.
- Move any fully defrosted stock that will not be used immediately, into a refrigerator or cold-room.
- Prepare the float for the point of sale.
- Switch on any equipment that needs to heat up.
- Do a roll call and morning briefing to ensure that all staff members on shift are fully aware of anything significant planned for the day, as well as any set targets.
- Ensure the briefing is minuted and signed by all staff present, confirming that all cleaning schedules have been assigned for the shift.
- Assign staff to daily preparation duties and monitor throughout the preparation.
- Confirm the store interior cleanliness and readiness to receive customers.
- Confirm the store exterior cleanliness, ensuring that all branding is clean and in full repair.
- Do final store walk-through, assessing all sections one more time.

- Open doors to trade.
- Ensure that all paperwork from the previous shift has been filed, and that a daily stock count was completed properly before the End of Day procedure was run on the Point of Sale.
- Verify the previous shift's banking. Always ensure that you do not do the banking every day at the same time if you don't make use of a cash collection service.
- Assess the previous shift's stock counts, noting any discrepancies or problematic areas that need to be discussed with that shift leader.

PRODUCTION PLANNING

Production Planning is one of the most important functions you and your management team will perform daily. Initially this will be very much a guessing game, but as time goes on and you accumulate data through daily transactions, this process will become easier and more accurate. However, common sense should not be left by the wayside.

Using your POS system's reporting functions, you can:
- Analyse historic trends
- Determine what average quantities of stock to have available at any given time and
- Plan your ordering.

As time goes by, you will get to know your business, and this will become second nature.

You should also use this information to determine your defrosting but remember to always defrost slightly more than the numbers indicate, since you may end up using more than you planned.

Remember to keep an event calendar. This is a useful tool to have. You may not always remember the reason why your business performed to a certain level when an appreciable amount of time has passed . Being able to refer to that time to see what incidents occurred or what unusual factors where involved, can help you make an informed decision.

Incidents such as protest action or factors such as power failures or water shortages can adversely affect trading. Understanding that these events are not likely to repeat exactly one year later or even 30 days from now, will help you to make better decisions when planning your defrosting or ordering.

DEFROSTING FROZEN PRODUCT

When defrosting frozen food, there are two factors that need to be considered:
- Temperature
- Time

The optimal temperature range for frozen product is between -18° to -20° Celsius (-0.4 to -4 ° Fahrenheit). For refrigerated stock the range is between 0° Celcius and 4° Celcius (32 to 39.2 ° Fahrenheit).

A functional probe thermometer is an extremely important piece of equipment that should be used daily in various aspects of ensuring food safety.

To begin with, frozen food by itself is not unsafe. However, if uncooked and raw, it has the potential to become unsafe. Microbes and bacteria do not necessarily die when frozen, and as the temperature of the food increases, these microbes and bacteria can become active again. Under the wrong circumstances they can cause the food to become a health hazard.

When food stock is approaching the end of the defrosting cycle, you need to carefully monitor the internal and external temperatures using a thermometer, to ensure that the stock is not exposed to unnecessary health risks by staying out too long before either being refrigerated or cooked. Once the stock item's core temperature reaches around – 5° Celsius (or 23° Fahrenheit), it should be refrigerated to complete the final defrosting in a refrigerated environment.

THE DEFROSTING PROCESS

If you are a franchisee, the franchisor will describe its own defrosting techniques.

Different types of stock are defrosted using different techniques. Depending on what the product is, you may want to seek advice from the supplier on the best possible defrosting method.

To ensure the fastest possible defrosting cycle turnaround time, try to ensure that there is enough air flow between the product pieces.

Any stock that has the potential to become harmful at room temperature must remain covered or sealed away from the atmosphere and must be allowed to thaw in a cool area to limit the possibility of contamination.

Chicken and fish are especially susceptible to contamination and if handled incorrectly, can cause salmonella or E.coli-related food poisoning.

Pork and red meat are highly susceptible to E.coli-related food poisoning, and pork-related products especially should be handled with care as pork is also highly susceptible to listeria.

Thawing times will depend on the type of product, the packaging, the weight and the defrosting procedure used.

You should never defrost any meat products in water, as this:
- Damages the texture and quality of the product
- Is highly unhygienic and dangerous, and
- Is also an indication of insufficient production planning.

HOLDING TIMES

Holding times are extremely important if you want to ensure that you deliver a quality and (above all) safe product to your customers. From frozen to defrosted, to cooked, there are rules to be taken very seriously. Defrosted stock must be cooked within 48 hours or be discarded. You cannot freeze the stock again, as this can cause serious contamination issues as well as affect the quality of the stock.

As a rule of thumb, cooked meat has a very limited holding time and should never be held over for sale from one day to the next. Not only will doing so seriously affect the quality and taste of the product, but very real health concerns are created.

Red meat, once cooked, should not exceed a hot holding time of more than 2 hours. Hot holding means the internal temperature of the product as measured with a probe thermometer should be between 50° Celsius and 60° Celsius (or between 122° and 140° Fahrenheit). A lower temperature will not inhibit bacteria growth enough and a higher temperature will cause the meat to cook further and dry out rapidly.

Fish, chicken and pork carry inherently more dangerous risk factors. Fish and chicken are both highly susceptible to Salmonella growth and should not be held for more than 60 to 90 minutes with a core temperature of 50° Celsius to 60° Celsius (or between 122° and 140° Fahrenheit) internal temperature as determined by a probe thermometer.

Pork is also a dangerous product to hold for too long as it is susceptible to various bacteriological factors. For safety, limit hot holding times to no more than 60 minutes at an internal temperature of 50° Celsius to 60° Celsius (or between 122° and 140° Fahrenheit).

STORAGE AND LABELLING

Any organic stock that requires refrigerated holding before use, must be stored in sealed containers that are labelled and dated, indicating the production or dispensing date as well as the expiry date. Whether premade or used as is, organic refrigerated stock that has been removed from its packaging or has been exposed to the open air must be used within 72 hours, after which it needs to be discarded.

Chicken Fillets

DD: 01/02/2018 ED: 03/02/2018

The label example above has the name of the product in the container, the Decanting Date and the Expiry Date. Great care should be taken to ensure that you never top up with new stock since this can cause cross-contamination. Always use a different, clean container for new stock and provide a new label for this container.

The principle of First In, First Out should always be applied, and this should be the case with all the organic stock in the store, including soft drinks and other canned or bottled goods.

COLD CHAIN AND TEMPERATURE CONTROLS

Common bacterial pathogens:

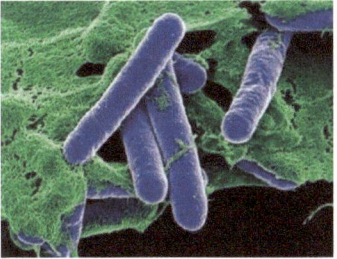

Clostridium botulinum bacteria grows on food and produces toxins that, when ingested, cause paralysis. Botulism poisoning is extremely rare, but so dangerous that each case is considered a public health emergency. Studies have shown that there is a 35 to 65 percent chance of death for patients who are not treated immediately and effectively with botulism antitoxin.

In early 2018, an Irish farmer lost 20 cows due to Botulism carried by poultry litter. Fortunately, this incident did not result in infected meat entering the food industry.

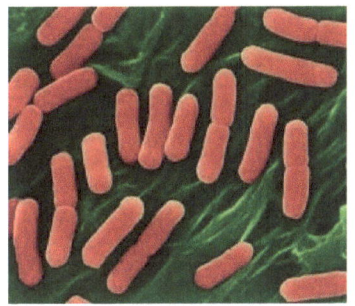

Escherichia coli - Most E. coli strains are harmless, but some types can cause serious food poisoning in their hosts and are occasionally responsible for product recalls due to food contamination. E. coli is expelled into the environment within fecal matter.

In early 2018, a whole range of dogfood had to be recalled by the manufacturer in the US, due to E. coli in the product.

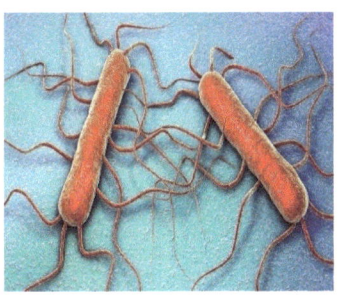

Listeria *L*. monocytogenes can cause a variety of symptoms ranging from mild flu-like, fever and gastroenteritis which can progress to the symptoms associated with the severe disease listeriosis. Infection occurs almost exclusively from the consumption of contaminated food stuffs. The bacterium is inactivated by heat, so standard cooking and pasteurization procedures will protect consumers from the possibility of infection.

In 2018, there was an outbreak of Listeria in a factory in Hungary. This factory exported maize (corn) to South Africa, where the maize was added to a spicy rice mixture for a top retail chain. The spicy rice mixture was recalled, and other products in various countries were also affected.

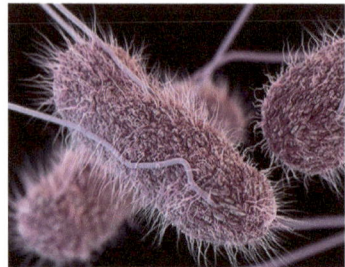

Salmonella has many possible sources of a salmonella infection:

Meat: Some of our favorite proteins to cook and eat have the bacteria. They include poultry (chicken, turkey, or duck), beef, veal and pork.

Fertilizer: The most common way to get salmonella is by eating meat or eggs or drinking milk that's contaminated. But you can also get it by eating fruits or vegetables that have been in contact with manure from animals that have salmonella.

In early 2018, a US grocery chain had to recall pasta salad made from salmonella infected eggs in eight states.

These common bacteria types can be controlled by simply following proper preparation methods, but more importantly through maintaining the **Cold Chain**.

A cold chain or cool chain is a temperature-controlled supply chain. An unbroken cold chain is an uninterrupted series of refrigerated production, storage and distribution activities, along with associated equipment and logistics, which maintain a pre-determined low-temperature range. The cold chain is used to preserve, extend and ensure the shelf life of products, such as fresh agricultural produce, frozen food and chilled products. Such products, during transport and when in transient storage, are sometimes called cool cargo.

Unlike other goods or merchandise, cold chain goods are perishable and always en route towards an end use or destination, even when held temporarily in cold stores. Therefore, a cold chain is commonly referred to as cargo during its entire logistics cycle.

If a cold chain is interrupted, for any reason, the natural bacteria found in all foodstuffs can begin to multiply and therefore pose a health risk. It is also for this same reason that any frozen product that has been defrosted once cannot be frozen again and must be used as soon as possible.

HYGIENE PRACTICES

Throughout the day your hands are constantly accumulating germs and bacteria from the surfaces and objects you touch. Infecting yourself is as easy as touching your eyes, nose or mouth, and you can easily spread the infection to others. It's impossible to keep your hands germ-free but washing your hands frequently can substantially help to reduce how much bacteria is transmitted.

In the QSR environment, it is recommended that each staff member wash their hands once every half hour at a minimum. This will prevent bacteria from multiplying to dangerous levels.

Remember to always wash your hands before:
- Preparing food or eating.
- Treating wounds or caring for a sick person.
- Inserting or removing contact lenses.

Always wash your hands after:
- Preparing food.
- Using the toilet or changing a diaper.
- Touching an animal, animal feed or waste.
- Blowing your nose, coughing or sneezing.
- Treating wounds or caring for a sick person.
- Handling garbage.

Also, wash your hands when they are visibly dirty.

Don't use antibacterial soaps. Antibacterial soaps are no more effective at killing germs than is regular soap. Using them can, over time, lead to drug and antimicrobial-resistant bacteria. These, like drug-resistant TB, then become much harder to fight.

HOW TO WASH YOUR HANDS

It's generally best to wash your hands with soap and water. Follow these steps:

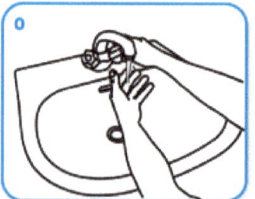
Wet hands with water

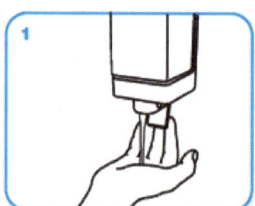
apply enough soap to cover all hand surfaces.

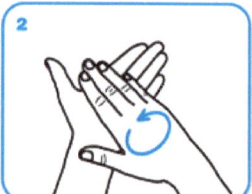
Rub hands palm to palm

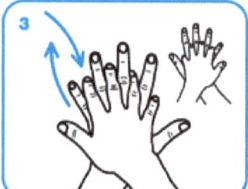
right palm over left dorsum with interlaced fingers and vice versa

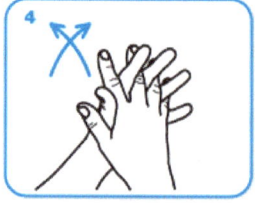
palm to palm with fingers interlaced

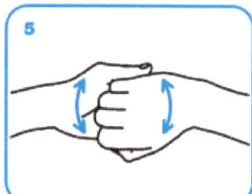
backs of fingers to opposing palms with fingers interlocked

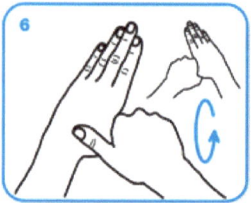
rotational rubbing of left thumb clasped in right palm and vice versa

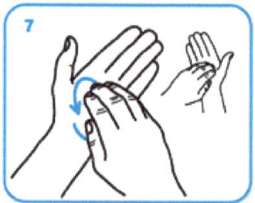
rotational rubbing, backwards and forwards with clasped fingers of right hand in left palm and vice versa.

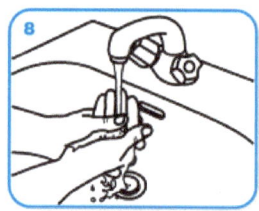
Rinse hands with water

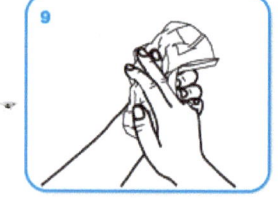
dry thoroughly with a single use towel

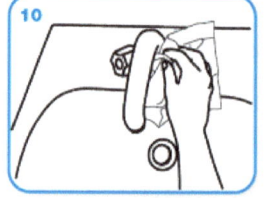
use towel to turn off faucet

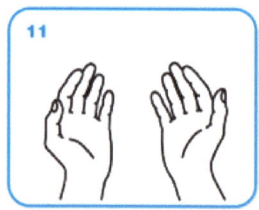
...and your hands are safe.

- Wet your hands with running water — either warm or cold.
- Apply liquid, bar or powder soap to a cupped hand.
- Lather well.
- Rub your hands, palm to palm, vigorously for at least 20 seconds. Remember to scrub all surfaces, including the backs of your hands, wrists, between your fingers and under your fingernails.
- Rinse well.
- Dry your hands with a clean towel.
- Use the towel to turn off the faucet.

HOW TO USE AN ALCOHOL-BASED HAND SANITIZER

Alcohol-based hand sanitizers, which don't require water, are an acceptable alternative when soap and water aren't available. If you use a hand sanitizer, make sure the product contains at least 60 percent alcohol.

Follow these steps:
- Apply enough of the product to the palm of your hand to wet your hands completely.
- Rub your hands together, covering all surfaces, until your hands are dry.

PROTECTIVE GEAR

Hair nets are essential. The last thing you want is a complaint about a hair in a customer's food. Staff must always wear hair nets and must cover all hair, regardless of any other headwear worn. Men with facial hair must wear beard nets as well, but it is much preferable to have them clean shaven when at work.

Any employee working directly with food should wear gloves. Normal disposable plastic gloves are fine. If you prefer to use the more durable but more expensive latex alternatives, please ensure that you choose the non-powdered gloves.

Uniforms are important to the image of any brand and business. However, in the QSR industry, there are more than just aesthetic considerations. Besides ensuring that you employees wear clean uniforms that are in good repair and not faded, frayed or worn, you should also ensure that they are made from non-flammable or flame-retardant materials. In this industry you will invariably work with either gas flame, hot oil or both , so safety is important.

All employees, including management must at all times wear closed, comfortable shoes with non-slip soles and their uniforms must cover as much of the lower extremities as possible. Always remember that we are working with heat. Any accidental spill of hot liquid such as oil or boiling water can cause serious injury and the correct footwear and clothing can go a long way to minimizing these injuries.

COLOR CODING

It is advisable to use the color-coding system that is commonly provided by equipment suppliers. Knives, cutting boards, chemical buckets and cleaning equipment are all available in color codes that indicate their use and you should ensure that your staff are well trained in their use, as they will substantially reduce the risk of cross-contamination.

Cutting boards and knives are commonly divided into the following colors:
- Blue – Seafood
- White – Bread
- Brown – Cooked and processed meats
- Green – Vegetables
- Yellow – Poultry
- Red – Red meat

Cleaning equipment such as brooms and mops for use in the QSR industry are commonly divided into three colors. Again, it is essential that these pieces of equipment only be used in their designated areas and for the purpose that they are coded for as this will prevent cross-contamination.
- Green – Common areas such as dining areas
- Yellow – For use in the kitchen and cooking areas
- Red – For use in customer toilet facilities

CLEANING SCHEDULES AND SAFETY

Cleaning schedules are extremely important. Not only do they help to maintain the image and condition of the store, but they serve to maintain hygiene. There are three very important cleaning schedules to implement: a Daily Cleaning Schedule, a Weekly Cleaning Schedule and the Extraction

Cleaning Schedule.

The Daily Cleaning Schedule should encompass the kitchen and all equipment, and most equipment suppliers will provide free training as a standard when they sell the equipment. It is incredibly important that the training be taken to heart, as it will ensure that your warranties are honored and that your equipment remains intact and in working condition as long as possible. The Daily Cleaning Schedule should also include an hourly cleaning schedule if you have customer toilet facilities on the premises as customers will absolutely judge you and your entire operation based on its condition.

The Weekly Cleaning Schedule should encompass every aspect of the daily cleaning schedule and should extend to the harder to reach areas such as the wall surfaces behind equipment, the inside of the cooler and freezer rooms, as well as the dry store.

The Extraction Cleaning schedule should be implemented daily. The extraction canopy must be installed no higher than 2 meters off the floor at its highest point, so that it can be effective in capturing condensate and is easily reachable for cleaning. Each removable filter must be cleaned individually using an effective degreasing agent. Since these filters are usually made from stainless steel, they can be soaked overnight, rinsed off and dried in the mornings and replaced before the equipment is switched on.

The extraction system, by law, must also be fully serviced and cleaned by a qualified servicing company at a minimum every six months and a servicing certificate must be issued indicating the next servicing date. The service must not only include the filters and the extraction canopy, but also the extraction ducting all the way from the canopy to the terminator at the end of the ducting on the outside of the building or on the roof.

Understand that the extraction, though seemingly harmless, is anything but harmless. When you use a gas grill to grill meat products, some of the fat contained in the meat evaporates, rises with the heat and condensates as it cools on the inside of the canopy and extraction ducting. When you use frying oil such as with chip fryers or pressure fryers the same happens with the cooking oil, whether palm based or sunflower based. These fats and oils are extremely flammable and will line the ducting along its entire length over time, which in the event of a fire will cause it to act like a candle wick.

I once had the unfortunate experience to be called out to a store that had caught fire due to a gas valve that had not been closed properly at the end of the day and a spark from a light fitting had set it alight. This store was scheduled to have its extraction system serviced and cleaned in less than a week. Had the servicing been done sooner, the extent of the damage would probably have been limited to the inside of the store. As it was, the extraction system caught fire and as a result the entire 5-story building caught ablaze. Luckily no-one was harmed as these upper floors contained only offices and were empty at the time. However, it could have been a lot worse.

Failing to properly service and maintain your extraction system can not only void any insurance you may have but could lead to criminal charges should there be extensive loss of property, serious injury or even death because of negligence.

Fire safety is a massive concern in the QSR industry. Not only should you have a fire evacuation plan prominently displayed near all access points, but you and your staff should also be fully aware of what each of you must do in the case of a fire. Regular discussion of such an event should be included in pre-shift briefings and should include:

- The use of fire extinguishers, safety blankets and first aid
- Each section's evacuation duties and
- Where the nearest evacuation points are.

If you are in South Africa, considering South Africa's politically volatile nature, you should also have in place plans to deal with an armed robbery or protest action turned riot. Your nearest police station should be able to assist in this kind of training.

Also ensure that you have an easily accessible list of emergency phone numbers for the nearest ambulance service, fire department, armed reaction or sector police.

CASH CONTROL AND FLOAT PRESERVATION

The process of cashing up is often made more difficult and confusing than it should be. There are a few things that you can do to make the process streamlined, effective and accurate.

Float is the money, broken down into various denominations from the smallest to the largest as is commonly used, to populate the till and make the sales. At the beginning this will be a learning exercise, but you should always ensure that you have enough backup float to cover each till 3 times over. You should also ensure that you always issue the exact same float to each till and cashier and that they verify the value of the float and sign for it on receipt. This will ensure that there is no dispute later.

Every cashier must be trained to verbally verify the denomination and value of the payment they receive from the customer for each transaction as well as the value of the change returned so that there is no reason for the customer to dispute it later. Often dishonest customers will use the lack of this process to swindle an unaware cashier with counterfeit currency or by claiming that the denomination given was larger than it really was, leaving them to answer the shortage at the end of the day.

This practice also keeps your cashiers honest and they should be questioned if they are caught not abiding by this rule. Should there be cause due to suspicion or customer complaint, the manager must perform a full cashing up on the cashier to verify the contents and to determine if there is a reason for concern.

The process of cashing up should be done with float preservation in mind. Float preservation is the process of retaining as much of the float, from the smallest denomination upwards for reuse later. When you begin a cashing up, you must ensure that the relevant cashier is present to verify everything is done above board, again to prevent any allegations of misconduct later.

Always start with the smallest denominations and work your way up until you have retrieved the full value of the initial float issued. You should then count the remaining currency in the till and verify it against the value the POS system indicates you should have based on the transactions performed during the cashier's shift. Never allow cashiers to share a till, as they will often blame each other for any shortages or inconsistencies.

I advise using a procedure called AOD, or Admission of Debt, to deal with any shortages or overages. The Admission of Debt is a form on which any shortages or overages are recorded. Any overages will need to be explained and must be treated with the same seriousness as any shortages. Cashiers must not benefit from any overages recorded.

The AOD procedure must also be included as a stipulation in the employment contract and each AOD must be signed by both the manager and the cashier on issue, to ensure that you, as the employer, are legally allowed to reclaim any losses from their salaries.

Not only will this go a long way to ensuring that the cashier takes the best possible care when dealing with customers and transactions, but it will allow you to evaluate their performance on a regular basis. Dishonesty cannot be allowed under any circumstances by anyone in your employ.

Remember to file all paperwork pertaining to the cashing up securely and to keep all records for a minimum period of at least one year. Also, take great care when you do the banking and deposits to vary the times if you do not make use of a cash collection service. Most robberies and thefts are usually based on insider information or careless talk.

STAFF INCENTIVES

Staff incentives are sometimes a difficult and contentious subject, but in my opinion goes a long way towards cultivating the growth of your business. Cashiers, supervisors and managers should be trained in the art of upselling, body language and effective communication skills and should be made to feel pride in their accomplishments.

Never discuss the day's trading budget with your staff or give them monetary targets. Often, doing so can be very dangerous should any staff discuss them outside the work environment. Criminal elements often make use of inside information to determine if a business is a suitable target for a robbery and how much cash they can expect to find on the premises.

Whenever you implement targets, do so using sales targets based on specific products and sales quantities. Every decent POS system has a reporting system that will allow you to monitor and quantify individual sales. You can implement monetary incentives or other rewards based on these.

SPECIAL OFFERS BASED ON SWOT ANALYSIS AND STOCK REPORTS

Implementing localized special offers is the lifeline of any independent and small QSR concern and should be done with the help and knowledge of your franchisor if you are a franchisee. Use your POS system's reporting to do a trend analysis based on each month's trading. Determine what your top 10 sellers are and create special offers based on these.

Never implement more than one local special offer at a time and never for more than 2 months at a time. Any longer than that and a special offer will no longer be considered a special offer. It will then become more of a detriment than a bonus and will begin to adversely affect your bottom line.

Regularly changing and bringing in new specials will keep your customers interested and coming back for more. You can also track your specials daily and use them as part of your incentives program.

If you have access to the franchisor's matrix or you have compiled your own, then you can use it to log the sales of each product for the previous month if you have yet to complete a full trading year, or for a comparable period for the previous year.

Use your stock reports to determine your top 20 best selling menu items as well as your bottom 10 menu items. Based on these you can build specials that are made up of those menu items your customers most demand

CLOSING CHECKLIST

- Ensure that all invoices received during the day have been captured on to the Point of Sales system.
- Ensure that all wastage has been recorded and accounted for.
- Ensure that all final customers have been served and left the store before closing and locking the front door.
- Cash up the cashiers.
- Complete daily/weekly stock count as per the procedure provided by the franchisor or as described previously.
- Confirm that all cleaning schedules have been completed and that all pertinent areas have been restocked, ready for the next day's trade – remember, if you are not happy, then it isn't done.
- Ensure that all equipment have been switched off as required.
- Ensure that production planning is in place for the next day (See the section titled Production Planning above).
- Do a final walk around the store to confirm that all areas are clean and that all equipment have been safely switched off.
- Switch off the lights and leave the store.
- Lock the front door.

CONTRIBUTIONS

CHRIS COOK

With 25 years QSR experience Chris Cook is quite the authority in the industry. For 10 years Chris worked for KFC as a Market Manager, looking after 230 Restaurants, 25 franchisees and 15 direct reporting subordinates.

Chris was also responsible for KFCs Zimbabwe, Botswana, Mozambique, Namibia and South African coastal markets. He also market-mapped Maputo and ensured that all their stores remained profitable after more than 12 years in their original locations.

Chris led the Africa project to scope out the sub-Saharan African regions for KFC, including countries such as Nigeria, Kenya, Tanzania, Zambia, Mozambique, Uganda, Angola.

He founded the Champion Chicken franchise and opened a total of 14 franchises over 10 years, including a corporate store in the Pinetown bus rank, which he sold to KFC after 5 years.

He then joined True Blue Foods as COO and looked after the largest KFC franchise with a total of 100 stores under his supervision.

In 2017 he joined Chicken Xpress as COO, shareholder and director and is now the owner of Chicken Xpress Hammersdale.

ELSABE SMIT

Elsabe Smit is a veteran publisher and contributed to the editing and layout.

REFERENCES

LSM
http://www.saarf.co.za/lsm-presentations/2012/LSM%20Presentation%20-%20February%202012.pdf

CLOSTRIDIUM BOTULINUM
http://www.foodborneillness.com/botulism_food_poisoning/

ESCHERICHIA COLI
https://en.wikipedia.org/wiki/Escherichia_coli

LISTERIA L. MONOCYTOGENES
https://www.biocote.com/blog/understanding-the-threat-of-listeria-monocytogenes/

SALMONELLA
https://www.webmd.com/food-recipes/food-poisoning/what-is-salmonella#1

www.ingramcontent.com/pod-product-compliance
Lightning Source LLC
Chambersburg PA
CBHW040324220526
45473CB00009B/2559